汉语桥－中学生夏令营
Chinese Bridge Summer Camp for Foreign Students

中国欢迎你 Welcome to China 短期汉语系列教材

国家汉办／孔子学院总部
Hanban / Confucius Institute Headquarters

You Henan

游河南

Welcome to Henan

地域类

高等教育出版社·北京
HIGHER EDUCATION PRESS BEIJING

“中国欢迎你”短期汉语系列教材

前言

随着中国与世界各国距离的拉近，越来越多的人渴望了解中国、体验中国。为了帮助“汉语桥”夏令营中小学生以及所有对中国感兴趣的外国朋友在较短时间内了解中国的语言和文化、历史与风俗，中国国家汉办/孔子学院总部组织研发了《中国欢迎你》短期汉语系列教材。

◉ 适用对象

本系列教材主要适用于来华参加夏令营的海外中小学生，也可用于海外孔子学院和孔子课堂作为汉语教学辅助资源。

◉ 教材构成

本系列教材分为三大类：语言类、才艺类和地域类。

《游河南》是地域类教材中的一册，主要介绍河南的地域文化和风土人情，包括少林寺、龙门石窟、清明上河园、中国文字博物馆、太极等。本书将地域文化的学习与参观游览有机地结合起来，同时配以丰富的练习和活动，目的在于让学习者在较短时间内了解河南、感知河南。本书的参考教学时间为6～8学时。

◉ 编写特色

1. 全新的编写理念：本系列教材借鉴了全新的外语教学理念和最先进的外语教学法成果，真正做到以学习者为中心，满足学习者的个性化需求。

2. 全新的编写风格：本系列教材话题实用，内容简单，形式丰富，图文并茂，寓教于乐，注重实效，目的在于使汉语变得“易懂、易学、易用”。

3. 全新的教学设计：本系列教材以任务和活动为主线，便于教师进行教学设计，充分调动学习者的兴趣，实现轻松有效的课堂教学。

让我们翻开书，一起去感知充满魅力的汉语和中国文化！

编委会

2011年5月

CONTENTS 目录

About Henan
河南简介

Henan, which is called "Yu" for short, is located in central China. Most of Henan's area is to the south of the Yellow River, so it is called "Henan." ("He" means "river," and "nan" means "south.") The capital of Henan province is Zhengzhou. The word "China" was first used to represent Henan, which was one of the earliest civilizations in China. China has had more than 20 dynasties with their capital in Henan, over a time span of 2 000 years. This long history and rich culture has given Henan many fascinating tourist sites: the Shaolin Temple, the Longmen Grottoes, and the Qingming Riverside Landscape Garden are all good places to visit.

河南简称"豫"，位于中国的中部，因大部分地区处于黄河以南而得名，省会是郑州市。"中国"一词最早就是指以洛阳为中心的河南一带，这里是中华文明和中华民族的发祥地之一。中国曾有20多个王朝在河南建都，历史跨越2 000多年。灿烂的历史文化为河南留下了丰富的旅游资源，少林寺、龙门石窟、清明上河园等都是值得游览的好去处。

The Shaolin Temple

少林寺

Warm-up 热身

1 Guess who practices kung fu at the Shaolin Temple.
猜一猜在少林寺里练功的是什么人。

① 僧人 (monk)　② 道士 (Taoist priest)　③ 牧师 (priest)

2 Do you know who these are? Please look at the pictures and match them with their corresponding names.
你知道他们是谁吗？请把图片和相应的名字连线。

Jackie Chan 成龙　　Jet Li 李连杰　　Bruce Lee 李小龙

Do You Know?

你知道吗？

The Shaolin Temple 少林寺

The Shaolin Temple is in Zhengzhou, the capital city of Henan province. Because it is located in the forest ("lin") of the Shaoshi Mountain, it is called the "Shaolin Temple." The Shaolin Temple is famous for its Chan Sect and its style of martial arts ("wushu") is known throughout the world. Now, the Shaolin Temple holds the "China International Shaolin Wushu Festival" every year, which attracts large numbers of martial arts enthusiasts from both China and the rest of the world to participate.

少林寺位于河南省郑州市，因其坐落在少室山下的丛林中，所以得名“少林寺”。少林寺以禅宗和武术并称于世。现在这里每年举办一次“国际少林武术节”，吸引了海内外众多的武术爱好者和武术团体前往参加。

Shaolin Kung Fu 少林功夫

In China, since ancient times, there has been a saying: "All kung fu came from Shaolin." The special characteristic of Shaolin kung fu is to combine the Chan Sect with kung fu. Monks practice kung fu to cultivate their moral characters and perfect their moral integrity. At the same time they also become physically stronger. Today, the word "Shaolin" has become an important symbol of Chinese traditional martial arts.

在中国，自古就有“天下功夫出少林”的说法。少林功夫的特点是禅武合一。僧众们练武是为了修身养性，同时也可以强身健体。如今，“少林”一词已经成为中国传统武术的重要象征。

Let's Think 想一想

1. Where is the Shaolin Temple?
   少林寺在哪里？
2. What is the special characteristic of Shaolin kung fu?
   少林功夫的特点是什么？

The Pagoda Forest 塔林

The Pagoda Forest is the ancient cemetery of the temple monks. The Shaolin Pagoda Forest is China's largest pagoda forest. In the Pagoda Forest, there are more than 230 ancient pagodas and each one's height, size, and number of levels are different. This is based on the prestige and merits of the monk before his death.

塔林是寺院中历代高僧的墓地。少林寺塔林是中国最大的塔林。塔林里有历代古塔230余座，每座塔的高低、大小和层数都不一样，这主要是根据少林和尚生前的威望和功德来决定的。

Pagoda Forest

At the back of your book, you can find sticker of the Pagoda Forest. Stick it in the correct place.

Useful Expressions 常用表达

1. 这是什么地方／招式？
   Zhè shì shénme dìfang / zhāoshì?
2. 您学功夫学了多长时间了？
   Nín xué gōngfu xuéle duō cháng shíjiān le?
3. 您可以教我两招吗？
   Nín kěyǐ jiāo wǒ liǎng zhāo ma?
4. 我做得对吗？
   Wǒ zuò de duì ma?
5. 这个寺院是什么时候建的？
   Zhège sìyuàn shì shénme shíhou jiàn de?

1. What is this place / pose?
2. How long have you been studying kung fu?
3. Can you teach me a couple of moves?
4. Am I doing it correctly?
5. When was this temple built?

Tasks 任务

1. When visiting the Shaolin Temple, please write down the name of the temple twice below.
参观少林寺的时候，请你抄写两遍牌匾上的寺名。

2. Find the largest building of the Shaolin Temple and write its name in the space below.
找一找少林寺中最大的殿宇，把它的名字写在下面的空格处。

3. Demonstrate two kung fu moves you learned at the Shaolin Temple. Then tell everyone the names of the moves. 在少林寺学两招少林功夫，给大家展示一下，然后告诉大家你学的招式叫什么名字。

The Longmen Grottoes

龙门石窟

Warm-up 热身

1. Guess which of the pictures below is the tallest Buddha statue in the Longmen Grottoes. Please tick the correct answer. 猜一猜下面哪个是龙门石窟中最高的佛像。请选择并画钩。

2. Guess how tall the tallest Buddha statue in the Longmen Grottoes is. How about the smallest one?
猜一猜龙门石窟中最高的佛像有多高。最小的呢？

A 17.14 meters, 0.02 meters
B 10 meters, 0.8 meters
C 107 meters, 0.1 meters
D 15.5 meters, 0.05 meters

Do You Know? 你知道吗？

Grottoes 石窟

Grottoes are a kind of temple architecture constructed by cutting into cliffs. In the cut-out place images or statues of Buddha are placed with murals that tell Buddhist stories and stone carvings. The earliest grottoes were developed following the increased interest in Indian Buddhism and later this practice came to China. Now China has four great grottoes which are: the Longmen Grottoes in Luoyang, Henan province; the Mogao Grottoes in Dunhuang, Gansu province; the Yungang Grottoes in Datong, Shanxi province; and the Maijishan Grottoes in Tianshui, Gansu province.

石窟是一种在山崖上开凿而成的寺庙建筑，里面通常有佛像或者关于佛教故事的壁画和石刻等。石窟艺术最早是伴随着印度的佛教而兴起的，后来传入中国。现在中国有四大石窟，分别是河南洛阳龙门石窟、甘肃敦煌莫高窟、山西大同云冈石窟和甘肃天水麦积山石窟。

the Longmen Grottoes

the Mogao Grottoes

At the back of your book, you can find stickers of the Mogao Grottoes and the Maijishan Grottoes. Stick them in the correct places.

the Yungang Grottoes

the Maijishan Grottoes

The Longmen Grottoes 龙门石窟

The Longmen Grottoes are in Luoyang, Henan province and they are one of China's four great grottoes. The Longmen Grottoes were under construction for 400 years. The first grottoes were carved more than 1 500 years ago. In the Longmen Grottoes, the biggest statue is a Buddha that is 17.14 meters (56 feet) high and the smallest one is only 2 centimeters.

龙门石窟，位于河南洛阳，是中国四大石窟之一。龙门石窟的开凿前后经历了400多年，最初开凿的一批石窟距今已有1 500多年的历史。龙门石窟中最大的佛像高达17.14米，最小的只有2厘米。

Why did ancient Chinese people call the Emperor "the True Dragon and the Son of Heaven?"

In ancient China, the dragon was considered as the Son of Heaven, a magical animal that could arouse the wind and rain and also a symbol of worship for the Chinese people. Common people thought that the Emperor and the dragon were the same — both were the Son of Heaven and held supreme power — so they called the Emperor "the True Dragon and the Son of Heaven."

为什么古代中国人把皇帝称为"真龙天子"？

在中国古代，龙被看做是天的孩子，是一种能兴风雨的神异动物，也是中华民族的图腾。百姓认为皇帝和龙一样，也是天的儿子，有至高无上的权力，所以称呼皇帝为"真龙天子"。

Activities 活动

Writing Chinese characters.

写汉字。

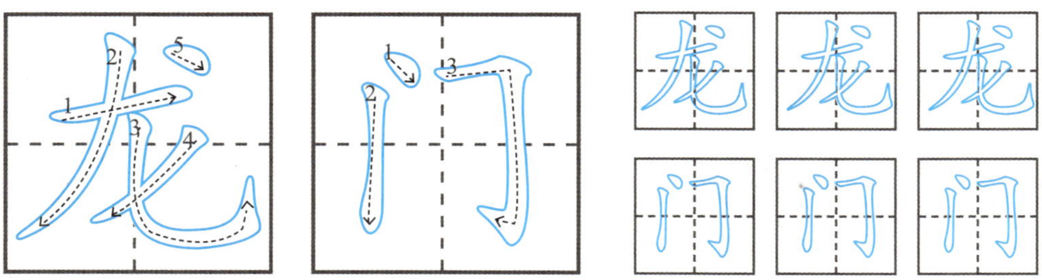

Useful Expressions 常用表达

1. 这尊佛像叫什么名字？
   Zhè zūn fóxiàng jiào shénme míngzi?
2. 它有多高？ 它有多少 年的历史了？
   Tā yǒu duō gāo? Tā yǒu duōshao nián de lìshǐ le?
3. 万佛洞离这里有多远？
   Wànfódòng lí zhèlǐ yǒu duō yuǎn?

1. What is the name of this Buddha?
2. How tall is it? How many years of history does it have?
3. How far is the Ten-Thousand Buddhas Cave from here?

Tasks 任务

1. Ask local people which was the earliest cave built in the Longmen Grottoes. Please write the name of it in the space below.
   问问当地人，在龙门石窟，哪个洞是最早开凿的？请将洞的名字写在下面的空格处。

2. When visiting the Longmen Grottoes, draw the Buddha that impressed you most and show it to your classmates.
   参观龙门石窟的时候，请把你印象最深的佛像画下来，向同学们展示一下。

The Qingming Riverside Landscape Garden

清明上河园

Warm-up 热身

1 Guess which of the following pictures is related to the Qingming Riverside Landscape Garden.
猜一猜下面哪幅画和清明上河园有关系。

①

②

③

2 Guess what they are doing.
猜一猜他们在干什么。

①

②

③

Do You Know? 你知道吗？

The Qingming Riverside Landscape Garden 清明上河园

Do you want to go back in time to see what China was like more than a thousand years ago? Well, why don't you come to the Qingming Riverside Landscape Garden? The Qingming Riverside Landscape Garden is in Kaifeng in Henan province and was built according to the design of the famous "Qingming Riverside Landscape Painting" in the Northern Song Dynasty. It recreates prosperous scenes of the Northern Song Dynasty (960—1127) capital city. Here, you not only can see the buildings of the Song Dynasty, but you can also enjoy street shows, unique folk performances, and traditional crafts. You can even taste many different kinds of local Kaifeng snacks.

你想回到1 000多前的中国去看看吗？那么请来清明上河园吧！清明上河园位于河南开封，是仿照北宋名画《清明上河图》中所绘场景而建造的公园，重现了开封作为北宋（960—1127）都城时的繁荣景象。在这里你不仅可以看到宋朝风格的城市建筑，还能欣赏到当时精彩纷呈的街头表演、民俗绝活和传统工艺，更能品尝到各种各样的开封小吃。

Let's Think 想一想

1. What was the Qingming Riverside Landscape Garden built according to?
   清明上河园是仿照什么而建造的公园？
2. Which dynasty does the Qingming Riverside Landscape Garden recreate?
   清明上河园再现的是中国哪个朝代的历史风貌？

The "Qingming Riverside Landscape Painting" 《清明上河图》

The "Qingming Riverside Landscape Painting" is one of China's ten most famous paintings to date. It is a nationally-treasured artefact, preserved in the Palace Museum in Beijing. It was painted by Zhang Zeduan, a famous artist during the Northern Song Dynasty. The content of the painting is abundant. It is painted with advanced techniques and it shows vividly the prosperity of Kaifeng and the lives of the people in the peaceful time of the Northern Song Dynasty.

《清明上河图》是中国十大传世名画之一，属于国宝级文物，现存于北京故宫博物院，作者是北宋画家张择端。这幅作品画面内容丰富，技法高超，生动地再现了北宋太平盛世时开封的繁华市景和民俗生活。

Activities 活动

Cuju (kickball) was China's ancient form of football which flourished during the Song Dynasty. It was one of the favorite sports of that time.

蹴鞠：是中国古代的足球运动，在宋朝时获得极大发展，是当时人们最喜爱的体育运动之一。

Maqiu (polo) was a sport played while horse-back riding and using a stick to hit the ball. It was one of the most popular sports during the Tang and Song Dynasties.

马毬：是一种骑在马上用杖击球的运动，是唐、宋时期最流行的球类运动之一。

Qiuqian (swing) was the favorite entertainment for girls of the Song Dynasty. There are many poems describing this pastime in the ancient China.

秋千：是宋朝时最受女子欢迎的娱乐活动，中国古代很多诗词中对此都有描写。

cuju

maqiu

At the back of your book, you can find stickers of *cuju* and *maqiu*. Stick them in the correct places.

Useful Expressions 常用表达

1. 这个表演太棒了！
   Zhège biǎoyǎn tài bàng le!
2. 他／她在做什么？
   Tā / tā zài zuò shénme?
3. 请问，这个多少钱？
   Qǐngwèn, zhège duōshao qián?
4. 你好，请问我能和你照张相吗？
   Nǐ hǎo, qǐngwèn wǒ néng hé nǐ zhào zhāng xiàng ma?
5. 我们去那边看看吧。
   Wǒmen qù nàbian kànkan ba.

1. That performance was wonderful!
2. What is he/she doing?
3. Excuse me, how much is this?
4. Hello, can I take a photo with you?
5. Let's go over there and have a look.

Tasks 任务

1. In the garden, ask some of the traditionally-costumed actors to take a photo with you.
   在清明上河园中与一位古装打扮的人照一张合影。

2. Taste at least one kind of snack. Write the name of it in the space below and introduce everyone as to what the snack is like.
   在园中品尝一种小吃，将小吃的名字写在下面的空格处，并向大家介绍一下。

The Museum of Chinese Characters

中国文字博物馆

Warm-up 热身

1. Think about which Chinese character the character archway in front of the Museum of Chinese Characters looks like.
看一看中国文字博物馆门前的字坊像哪个汉字。

A 家　　B 人　　C 字　　D 房

2. Look at the Chinese character "大" (dà, big) and see how it has changed over time.
让我们一起了解一下汉字"大"的演变过程。

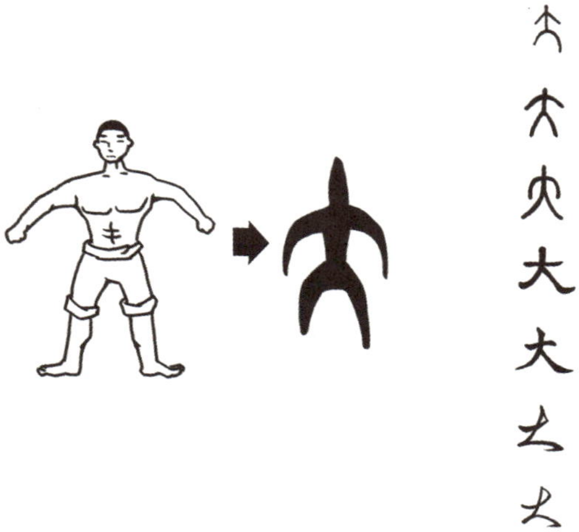

大 dà

Ancient Chinese considered people as the highest and the greatest of all the creatures in the universe, so the shape of a person came to represent "big."

中国古人把人看做万物之灵，是伟大的，所以用直立的人形表示"大"的意思。

Do You Know? 你知道吗？

The Museum of Chinese Characters is located in Anyang in Henan province. It is China's first Museum focusing on Chinese characters as its main theme. It contains 4 123 cultural relics, including *jiaguwen* (oracle bone script), *jinwen* (bronze script), *jiandu* (bamboo strips used for writing in ancient times), and *boshu* (books copied on silk.) The Museum of Chinese Characters uses the world's words as a background and uses Chinese characters as the main part. It also emphasizes the importance of the words and characters of Chinese ethnic minority groups, gathering together the best Chinese character symbols from each dynasty. You can learn about the changing process of Chinese characters and feel the splendor of Chinese characters and their culture.

中国文字博物馆位于河南省安阳市，是中国第一座以文字为主题的博物馆，共收藏文物4 123件，内容涉及甲骨文、金文、简牍和帛书等。中国文字博物馆以世界文字为背景，以汉字为主干，以中国少数民族文字为重要组成部分，荟萃历代中国文字的样本精华。你在这里可以了解中国古汉字的演变过程，感知灿烂的汉字文化和华夏文明。

Let's Think 想一想

1. Where is the Museum of Chinese Characters?
   中国文字博物馆在哪里？
2. How many cultural relics does the Museum of Chinese Characters contain?
   中国文字博物馆里有多少件文物？

Evolution of Chinese Characters 汉字的演变

oracle bone script 甲骨文 → bronze script 金文 → small seal script 小篆 → clerical script 隶书 → regular script 楷书 → cursive script 草书 → running script 行书

Activities 活动

Work in pairs and rearrange the four characters in each group below according to the evolution of their shapes.
两人一组，把下面每组的四个字按照汉字字形的演变顺序重新排列。

Useful Expressions 常用表达

1. 这是什么字？
Zhè shì shénme zì?
2. 这是哪个少数民族的文字？
Zhè shì nǎ gè shǎoshù mínzú de wénzì?
3. 这里的文物真多啊！
Zhèlǐ de wénwù zhēn duō a!

1. What (Chinese) character is this?
2. Which minority group does this writing come from?
3. There are so many cultural relics!

Tasks 任务

1. Find the character archway shown in the following picture and take a photo. Show your photo to your classmates.

参观时找到下图中的字坊，在它前边照一张相，向全班同学展示。

2. What materials were Chinese characters once written on? Please ask someone working at the museum, and then write the answer in the space provided.

中国古代的文字曾经写在哪些材质上面？请问问博物馆的工作人员，将答案写在下面的空格处。

Taiji

太 极

Warm-up 热身

1. Guess which of the following is a picture of *taiji*.
猜一猜下面哪张图片的内容是太极武术。

2. How much do you know about different types of *taiji*? Let's look at the pictures to learn more about them. 关于太极武术的种类，你知道多少？我们一起来看图了解一下吧。

taijiquan
太极拳

taiji with sword
太极剑

taiji with fan
太极扇

Do You Know? 你知道吗？

Taiji 太极

In ancient Chinese, the meaning of "*taiji*" is "the center of space." Ancient Chinese people used "*taiji*" to represent this process: from the center of the universe, chaotic states become spaces where a center point forms, following the process of creating life. *Taiji* is divided into two parts: the *yin* and the *yang*. All things and all phenomena in the world include *yin* and *yang*, which struggle against each other, depend on each other, and transform into each other. Now, the concept of "*taiji*" has become an important part of Chinese philosophy and culture.

"太极"在中国古文中的意思是"太空的中心"。中国古人用"太极"表示宇宙由无中心点的混沌状态变成有中心点的太空，随后化生万物的过程。太极分为阴、阳两个部分，而世界上的一切事物和现象也都内含阴阳，这两个部分相互斗争、相互依存、相互转化。现在，"太极"这一概念已成为中国哲学和文化的重要组成部分。

taiji

At the back of your book, you can find sticker of "*taiji*." Stick it in the correct place.

Let's Think 想一想

What is the meaning of "*taiji*" in ancient Chinese?
"太极"在中国古文中是什么意思？

Taijiquan 太极拳

Following the principles of *yin* and *yang* in *The Book of Changes*, integrating Taoist thinking, as well as the meridian lines of the body in traditional Chinese medicine, ancient people in China created an exercise called *taijiquan* that matches the physical structures of the human body to the movements of the natural world. *Taijiquan* is not only a type of kung fu, it is also a sport and a work-out. *Taijiquan* is characterized by "the blending of movement and stillness, strength and gentleness."

太极拳是中国古人依据《易经》中的阴阳之理，融合道家思想和中医经络学等创造出来的符合人体生理结构和大自然运转规律的拳术。太极拳既是一个武术派别，也是一项体育运动和健身运动，其主要特点是“动静结合、刚柔相济”。

Activities 活动

Writing Chinese characters.

写汉字。

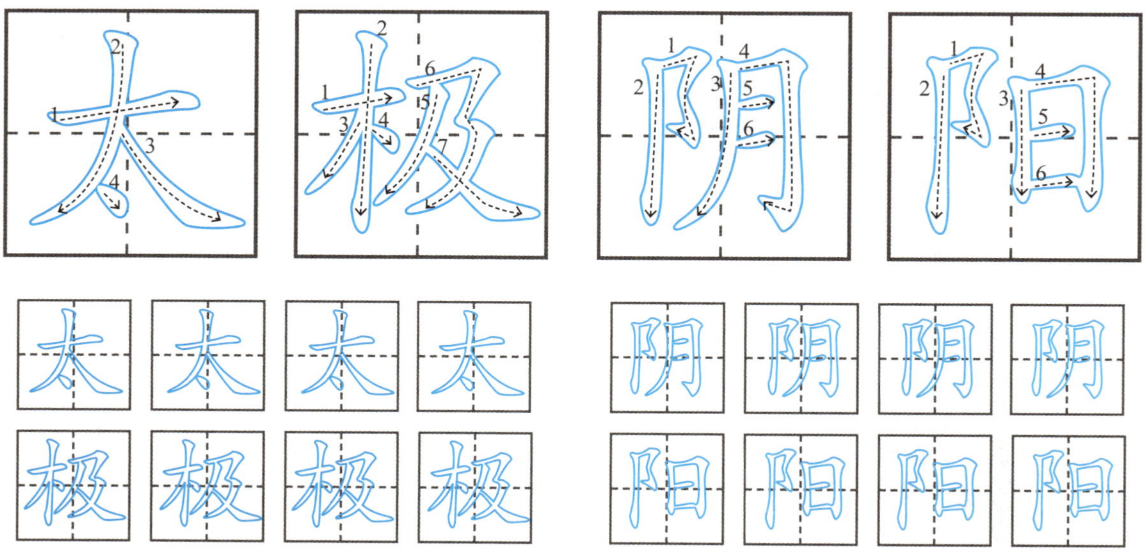

Useful Expressions 常用表达

1. 我想学习太极拳。你可以教我吗？
   Wǒ xiǎng xuéxí tàijíquán. Nǐ kěyǐ jiāo wǒ ma?
2. 是这样吗？我这样做对吗？
   Shì zhèyàng ma? Wǒ zhèyàng zuò duì ma?
3. 我给大家表演一下。
   Wǒ gěi dàjiā biǎoyǎn yíxià.

1. I want to learn *taijiquan*. Can you teach me?
2. Is this the way? Am I doing it right?
3. I will demonstrate for everyone.

Tasks 任务

1. Learn one *taijiquan* movement. Show it to your friends and explain to them how to do it.
   学一招太极拳招式，向朋友展示并讲解这个招式。

2. Take a photo of yourself practicing *taijiquan* and paste it in the space below.
   拍一张你正在练太极拳的照片，贴在下面的相框里。

Answers 答 案

The Shaolin Temple
少林寺

1. 

monk 僧人

2. 

成龙 Jackie Chan　李连杰 Jet Li　李小龙 Bruce Lee P2

1. The Shaolin Temple is in Zhengzhou, the capital city of Henan province. 少林寺位于河南省郑州市。
2. The special characteristic of Shaolin kung fu is to combine the Chan sect with kung fu.
   少林功夫的特点是禅武合一。 P3

2. The largest building of the Shaolin Temple is the Thousand Buddhas Hall.
   少林寺中最大的殿宇是千佛殿。 P5

The Longmen Grottoes
龙门石窟

1. 

2. A P6

1. The Guyang Cave. 古阳洞。 P9

The Qingming Riverside Landscape Garden
清明上河园

1. 

2. ① water transport 漕运
   ② throwing silk ball 抛绣球
   ③ making snacks 做小吃 P10

1. The Qingming Riverside Landscape Garden was built according to the design of the famous "Qingming Riverside Landscape Painting" in the Northern Song Dynasty. 清明上河园是仿照北宋名画《清明上河图》中所绘场景而建造的公园。
2. The Northern Song Dynasty. 北宋。 P11

The Museum of Chinese Characters
中国文字博物馆

1. C P14

1. In Anyang in Henan province. 河南省安阳市。
2. The Museum contains 4 123 cultural relics.
   中国文字博物馆共收藏文物4 123件。 P15

①
②
③
④

P16

Taiji
太极

1. 

P18

1. In ancient Chinese, the meaning of "*taiji*" is "the center of space." "太极"在中国古文中的意思是"太空的中心"。 P19

图书在版编目（CIP）数据

游河南 / 国家汉办 / 孔子学院总部编著. —北京：高等教育出版社，2011.7（2015.11 重印）
《中国欢迎你》短期汉语系列教材. 地域类
ISBN 978-7-04-032809-7

Ⅰ. ①游… Ⅱ. ①国… Ⅲ. ①汉语－阅读教学－对外汉语教学－教学参考资料 Ⅳ. ① H195.4

中国版本图书馆 CIP 数据核字（2011）第 111159 号

策划编辑 周 芳　责任编辑 金飞飞　封面设计 乔 剑　版式设计 悦尔视觉
插图选配 金飞飞　责任校对 金飞飞 李 桑　责任印制 朱学忠

出版发行 高等教育出版社
社 址 北京市西城区德外大街4号
邮政编码 100120
印 刷 北京信彩瑞禾印刷厂
开 本 787×1092 1/16
印 张 1.75
字 数 44 000
购书热线 010-58581118
咨询电话 400-810-0598
网 址 http://www.hep.edu.cn
http://www.hep.com.cn
网上订购 http://www.landraco.com
http://www.landraco.com.cn
版 次 2011 年7月第 1 版
印 次 2015 年11月第 3 次印刷
定 价 13.80元

物 料 号 32809-00